KINDER-KEYBOARD

Teacher's Manual

© Copyright 1977 by LEE ROBERTS MUSIC PUBLICATIONS, INC.

2301

CONTENTS

The music in *KINDER-KEYBOARD* is designed to provide early interrelated musical experiences with melody, harmony, and rhythm in various simple forms as necessary prerequisites for continued musical growth and enjoyment throughout life. The young child accumulates fundamental knowledge as he or she participates and experiments in a never-ending sequence of creative musical experiences. The only limit is the time that the teacher, student, and parents can make available. There is no quantitative limit to one's creative abilities or imagination.

Too much of today's educational practice stifles the creative potential of the child. The young child is too often overburdened with the processes of remembering a new series of words or learning to add columns of figures so that the intuitive aspects of his self are almost totally neglected. Here we have a chance to deal with individual differences as young students experiment with certain common knowledge, facts, and skills, which all can share and utilize. The students experience, discover, and explore broad musical concepts in preparation for eventual analysis and symbolization. The musical action always precedes verbalization.

Although pre-school children are not, as such, adept at skillful group interaction and, in fact, are quite often definitely self-centered, nonetheless the process of each child's discovering how to teach himself is the most effective and enjoyable way to assimilate knowledge. In effect, each child is *learning* how he or she can *learn*.

The piano is an ideal vehicle for acquiring the language of music via the three educational senses of sight, touch, and hearing. The children can see what they are doing both at the keyboard and on the printed page. They can reach out and touch the notes they are playing (going higher or lower, faster or slower, louder or softer, as they desire), and they can hear the various combinations of sonorities, including contemporary sounds along with those of yesteryears in an endless variety of activities to spark each child's creative imagination.

KINDER-KEYBOARD may be used as the pre-school keyboard instruction component of a private studio program or it may be used as the music program in a nursery school. It is expected that the teacher will use many songs of her own that she improvises with the children, as well as introduce interesting records for rhythmic activities as she sees fit. Where two classes of forty-five minutes each are scheduled per week, the teacher should have no trouble covering the materials in the book in approximately thirty-six weeks with review and related activities.

In your studio you should have a well-tuned piano and a lined chalkboard low enough so that pre-school children can reach both treble and bass clef without difficulty. In addition you should plan to have space for a bulletin board where children can gather around to look at the various items that have been placed on it. Additional equipment would include tape recorder, record player, filing cabinets, and low tables and chairs for young children. Also, it is suggested that you have a nearby closet where you can store your "props," such as flash cards, rhythm instruments, and other materials to be used throughout the year.

While the room should be arranged so the children can move freely to the keyboard without bumping into chairs and tables, try to arrange chairs, blackboard, etc., so that you can focus the children's attention in a fairly small area.

The teacher should consult *MUSIC FOR MOPPETS TEACHERS MANUAL* regarding testing and grouping children.

Parents must read and check the reservation form which stipulates that there will be no drop-outs during the year. This is very important in terms of formulating and maintaining good grouping. Likewise, they should understand how they are to participate at home with the child -- not as a disciplinarian enforcing a practice schedule, but rather as another member of the family who wants to share the fun and musical excitement that the child is experiencing. It is absolutely imperative that the parent have a well-tuned piano available for the child. If this is not available in the home, some practice arrangement should be made so the child has daily access to a piano.

Neither the child's book nor the teacher's manual are organized in units as was the case with *MUSIC FOR MOPPETS*. There is no need for the teacher to jump around in the book, since the learning sequence unfolds rather naturally and gradually. On the other hand, slight deviations, if deemed appropriate, should cause no problems. Of more importance is good, systematic review every few weeks to see if the students can use that which they have previously learned and apply it to new situations. Teachers must constantly strive for "transfer of learning," and not assume that this takes place automatically.

Twins and Triplets (page 2)

Much of the success in learning to play the piano hinges on the student's ability to see the groupings of two and three black keys in his mind as he feels them on the keyboard. Students should darken the Twins and Triplets on page 4 to facilitate this recognition process. Also you can draw "freehand" keyboards if additional experience seems necessary. In some cases, students might draw their own.

To practice the tactile development at home, students can reach out without looking at the piano keyboard and "feel" the Twins and Triplets. When they think they have found whichever group they are seeking, they can look at the keyboard to check themselves. Or they can do this as a game with another member of the family. Be sure they find them high and low on the keyboard in addition to the middle range.

One of the first activities for the children as a matter of orientation would be to march to music as they move around the room. Here are some ideas for improvising marching music.

(a)

It is essential that the children "feel" the beat, although this at first may be difficult for some of them. Do not confuse rhythm and beat. The beat is a steady on-going pulse, while the rhythm is the alternating long and short of the melody or harmony. It is suggested that you first have the children walk around the room as you play a simple ostinato of major and minor triads in the left hand and a simple melodic line in the right hand, similar to the examples above. Feel free to create a dissonant melodic line -- don't restrict it to the consonants of a I-V$_7$ chord progression. This marching activity can be used in an endless variety of ways including the exploration of soft and loud (crescendo and diminuendo) as children walk away from the piano or come closer. Also, the concepts of fast and slow, as well as high and low can be presented. This will be explored later in the book.

As specifically regards the Twins and Triplets, it is suggested that the teacher improvise some simple words with the children to chant over an ostinato on the black keys. They can march around the room as you first play the two black keys for them. Later on, the children can take turns playing the black keys anyplace on the keyboard. Of course, this is a great opportunity to deal with high and low.

(b) Twins

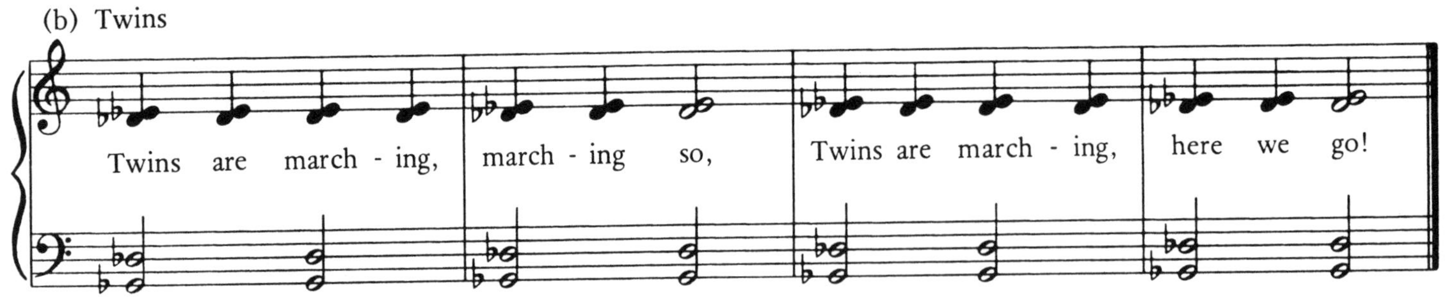

(c) Triplets

Following the short march with the Twins, the teacher should switch to the three black keys called the "Triplets." (See music on preceding page.) Again, she should make up a similar song for that activity.

The children should now be able to make up songs about the Twins and Triplets at home. The parents can provide a simple ostinato as the child creates new melodies, and hopefully, the child will want to play the ostinato as the parent tries his or her luck at improvising new Twins and Triplets marching songs.

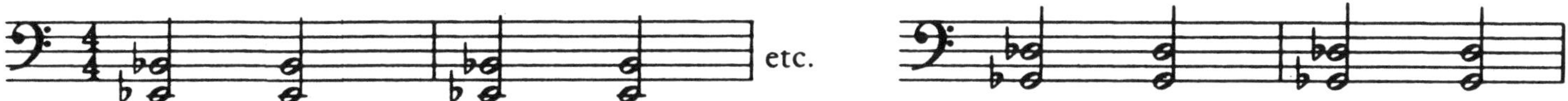

The following Twins and Triplets song deals with a more difficult melodic line. It is not suggested that the children will do anything as "fancy" as this at the first lesson; however, for its sound, it can be played and sung there and also be given to the parents for their information.

Marching Song

As previously suggested, a game of finding Twins or Triplets without looking at the hands on the keyboard (do it by feel) can be played at home by families. Students love to play Twins and Triplets "Hide and Seek." To introduce this in class, the teacher should have the student stand at the piano without touching it and look away as she asks for either the Twins or Triplets. The student must find them by touch without looking at the keyboard. The student raises his hand when he thinks he has found the correct one. Then he can look to see if he was correct.

Step and Hold (page 3)

The following procedure will be helpful in presenting new songs to the children. There are slight variations that add interest and variety, but essentially the same sequence should be used each time.

1) Sing and shape the melody in the air as the children follow along with you.
2) Repeat step 1 since the children will now have a better idea of what is coming.
3) Sing the melody a third time and clap the rhythm. Usually it is best for the children to walk the beat as they clap the rhythm. They may move around the room or walk in place.
4) Sample the keys to be used (in this case the three black keys), then let the children find their position and play the song.

Later, when students have gained some finger control, the following steps can be added:

5) Sing the melody again as you and the students simulate playing it in the air with your fingers.
6) Let the children play the melody on your arm or on their arm. This will help them get a feeling of transferring the weight from one finger to another. For children with minimal coordination, let them play the beginning tunes with one finger (the pointer) or the second and third fingers pressed together.

You may not need to repeat steps 1 through 4 if you are simply using the same song in the same key but changing from right to left hand or vice versa. After the students have played it in the first key in several positions on the piano (high and low), you may wish to transpose to adjacent keys. It may be good to continue to the next activity and come back for the transposition later on as a form of good review before the students leave.

Also, this little melody can be used as a *listening game*. The teacher can show the students how to make up new melodies on these three tones beginning on the top or middle tone. They can also begin on the bottom and skip up. To develop both responsiveness of the ear and the creative imagination of the student, they should be encouraged to make up as many little patterns as possible on these three black keys. And, of course, this can be a very interesting and exciting activity for parent and child to experience together.

Twins and Triplets   (page 4)

First let the students find the Twins high, middle, and low on the keyboard. Then let them darken each set of Twins on page 4. Follow the same procedures for Triplets. As a continuation of the tactile development begun on page 2, students should practice finding the Twins and Triplets without looking at their hands. This should be both part of the daily practice and also included in the lesson for several weeks.

Bees 'N' Bears   (page 5)

The text of this story is to be used as a point of departure to inspire other stories about various animals or happenings that may interest the children. And, of course, they should make up variations of their own on this particular story. Their variations should be kept short and limited to three or four characters. Each character should be given a motive or short theme as follows:

The motive should be sounded when that particular character is in action (*a la Peter and the Wolf*). Notice that Betty and Billy Bear's themes are very similar, since they are almost Twins. One must look and listen carefully to tell the difference.

STORY (you can make your own variations)

On the very edge of the big forest, a beautiful stream rippled on its way to the wide, wide ocean. A mamma bear with two curious cubs lived near an old hollow tree where honeybees made their home. Mamma knew the bees would get very angry if she took all of their honey. Maybe though, if she came at night while they slept and she borrowed only a little honey, they would not get so upset. So, on a nice moonlit night she decided to take a stroll to the old tree and reach into the hollow trunk where the honey was stored. Bzzzz. Bzzzz. Bzzzz. (Sleeping Bees motive.) The bees didn't like that one little bit, but then (bzzzz) they were sleepy, so (bzzzz) they went to sleep again and Mamma (Mamma theme) tiptoed back to her cubs with some honey for breakfast.

The next morning the cubs (theme) loved their treat and wanted more honey. Mamma (theme) said, "No, you must wait. The bees are awake and will be angry." That wasn't good enough for the two silly little cubs (theme), who said, "We are much bigger than those little, tiny bees and we aren't afraid of them." So, off they went to the tree. (Walking motive.) They couldn't quite reach the hole in the tree, however, so one cub (motive) stood on the other cub's (motive) shoulders.

The cub just started to reach in when -- Bzzzz, bzzzz, bzzzz. (Angry bee music.) OUCH! Bzzzz, bzzzz. (More angry bee music.) OUCH! OUCH! It seemed as though bees were coming from everywhere. The cubs fell head-over-heels ("falling" music [tone clusters]) as they tried to run to the stream, with all the bees right behind them. (Angry bee music.) Then, just for good measure, as the cubs tried to jump into the stream where the bees couldn't get them, the bees gave them one more good sting right where they sat down.

Finally, the bees went back to the tree (angry bee music getting softer), and the cubs saw Mamma (theme) standing on the opposite bank. She didn't say much because each time the cubs tried to set down, well, somehow they were reminded of her warning not to bother the bees.

That night as they went to bed they wondered, "How can we go back and get some more honey, but not make the bees so unhappy?" Well, what do you think?

Students and parents can make up two-line poems similar to this and improvise their own pentatonic tunes:

Two little bear cubs scrambled through the trees,
Two little bear cubs found some honeybees!

Here is an idea for a new melody:

Here is another melody with a "drone bass" accompaniment.

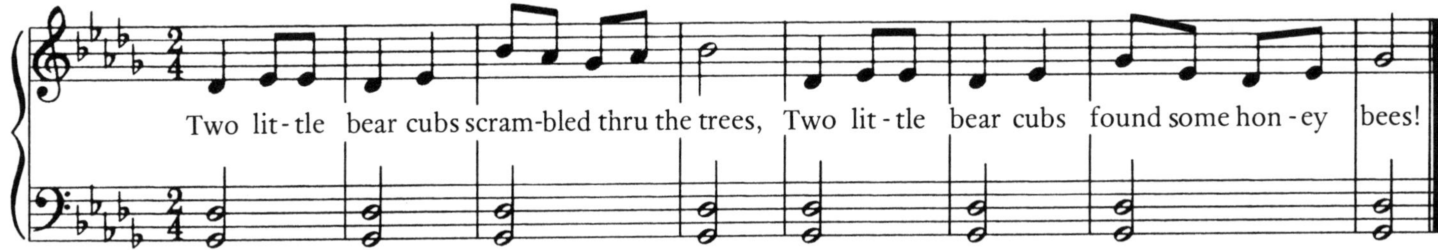

Duke of York   (pages 6 and 7)

This well-known folk tune is excellent for marching the beat as one claps the rhythm of the melody. The children can dramatize marching "up the hill" by starting in a crouching position. As they go up the hill they gradually stand erect, and as they go down the hill, they return once again to a crouching position. Here is the second verse, which is good for dramatizing up and down:

And when they were up, they were up; and when they were down, they were down;
And when they were only halfway up; they were neither up nor down.

Also, the song should be used to dramatize loud and soft as the soldiers march nearer or go off into the distance. The two examples of an ostinato bass shown here can provide a simple background for the marching song.

Later the children can provide their own accompaniment by playing the two tones together on the first of each measure. Eventually, some children may be able to play both the melody and the ostinato accompaniment. Finally, let the children improvise new melodies on these words and even new verses about the duke and his marching around the countryside. Here is an idea for another melody.

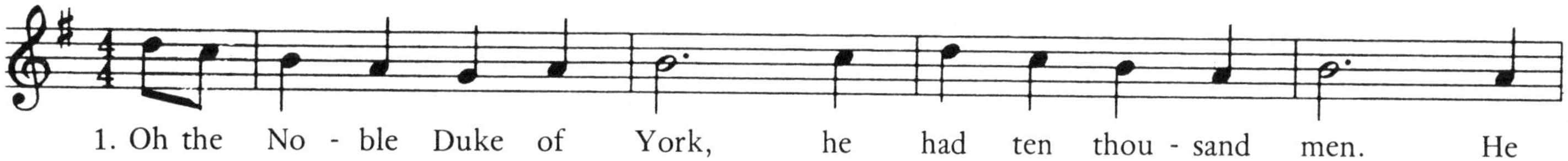

Musical Alphabet (page 8)

Some pre-school children already know the alphabet or at least are acquainted with certain letters of it. Although there is no stress on learning the alphabet per se, it is useful in finding the beginning positions of songs that will be played throughout the year. Ultimately the letter names will be applied to lines and spaces of the grand staff.

This activity may be introduced by the teacher chanting the first seven letters of the alphabet -- A B C D E F G -- and again repeating it several times as the children do this in a sort of rhythm.

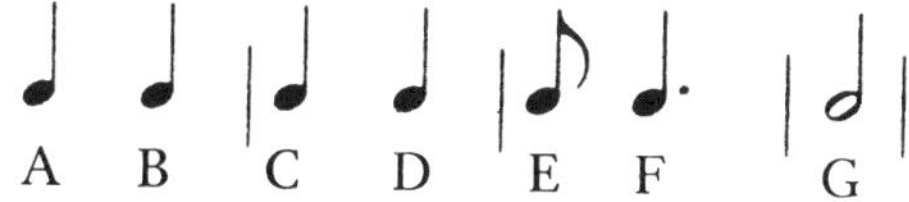

Next you might have the children sing this:

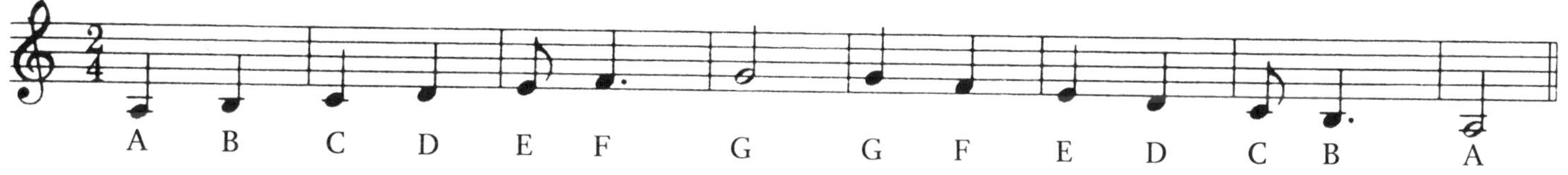

After the song, the teacher could have the children form a single line at the piano while she hides a note (A, B, C, etc.) for them and they try to find it. Also, the children can hide a note for her. In the beginning it would be best if they would hide a note close to A. Later they can expand it from A to A on the piano.

The teacher stands to one side and hides a note in the middle of the piano. The student has two chances to find this. If the student misses the first time, the teacher should play it a second time and have the other students help the one finding it and determine whether he or she was too high or low. After that student has had his turn he should go to the back of the line, and the same procedure is repeated with the next student.

It is advisable to drill on *Musical Alphabet* (A-through-G sequence) at the keyboard for a number of weeks. One or two children can try it at the piano with you, as the others chant the letter names. Then rotate and let two more children help you. At the parent lesson, be sure to show them how to play this game at home with their child.

After the student has developed some skill in finding the entire sequence from A to G, drill on shorter sequences such as A-B-C or B-C-D or C-D-E, etc. Also drill backwards from A such as A-G-F. A few minutes of this note-finding game at each lesson gives the children an opportunity to learn the letter names of the keyboard and is also fun.

Here is a suggested sequence for the keyboard drill:

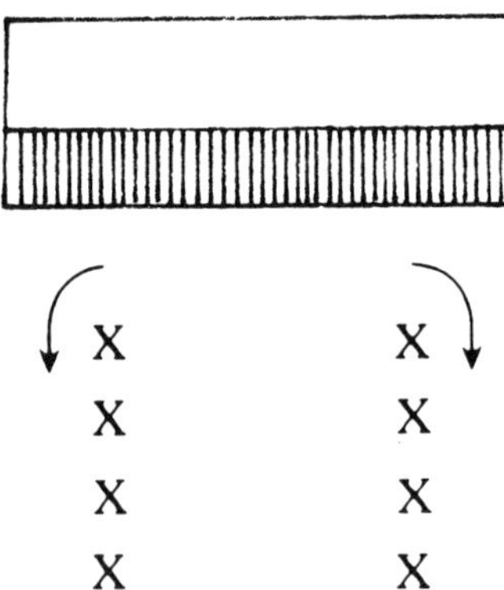

1) Students stand in two rows facing the piano. Teacher calls out "A" and students play that with pointer finger of either hand.
2) Teacher next calls out "B" and students quickly find that.
3) Next, the teacher calls out "A" or "C" as she desires, and the students again find that note.
4) Rotate with the next two students in the line and follow this same procedure.

After a few tries, students learn to be attentive and ready for their next turn at the keyboard. They can play this with a brother or sister at home or with a parent who needs to learn about sharps and flats.

Some studios are equipped with large floor keyboards. Children enjoy finding the ABCs on these by stepping on the key for the particular letter that was called out.

If the teacher feels that more work should be done on writing the letter names, she may ditto additional large keyboards to send home as worksheets. Be sure to show the parent and student how to complete these at home so that it is something they do quickly rather than becoming "busy work."

Question and Answer   (page 9)

This march-type melody provides a strong metric pulse for children experiencing their first musical "questions and answers." There should be four pulsations (not an accent, as such) in the question followed by four in the answer. Students may play the question and answer with either hand and may use only the pointer finger if dexterity is a problem. Let them hear you make up several answers to the first question to get the idea. Then have them create their own answers. Don't let them stop -- keep the beat going even if they simply play the same note throughout. Their answer should start with at least the first two notes of the question. Then they may change the rest of it in a variety of ways.

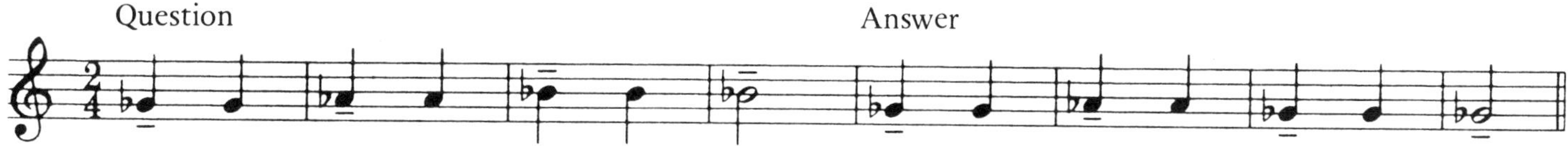

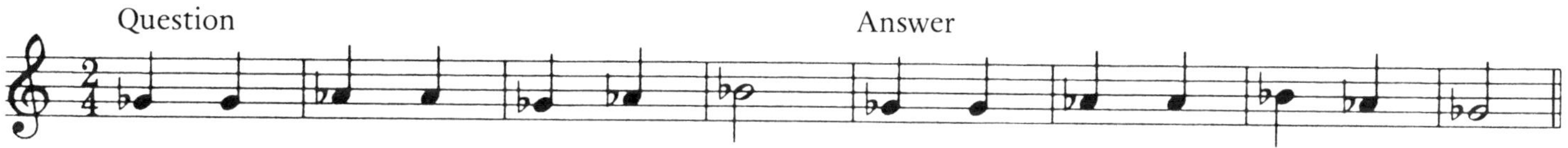

Once they have the idea, let them make up their own four-bar questions, then create their own answers. Of course, have them transpose to other keys. Again, in the early stages be sure that the student uses the motive of his question to begin his answer (called a *parallel period*).

Rocket to the Moon   (page 10)

Rocket to the Moon involves the following sequence:

1)   Getting ready for the trip.
2)   Countdown and blast-off.
3)   The flight through space and talking to earth.
4)   The moon landing.
5)   Weightless on the moon.
6)   Back to the ship and blast-off from the moon.
7)   Return trip to earth and a safe landing in our backyard.

Initially, the teacher can improvise music for the children to move around the room as they pretend they are getting things ready on their spaceship for blast-off. (Later, the students can improvise the music.) They must pack their things, check out the spaceship to make sure everything is in good order for the trip, and finally get in a crouched position on the floor for the countdown and blast-off.

Here is an idea for "busy music" (getting ready). Children's improvisations for this could be simply random sounds.

The countdown and blast-off should be ten, low, slow tones of equal duration and intensity, finally ending with a big tremolo-crescendo at the bottom of the keyboard, which gradually becomes a glissando upward to the mid range.

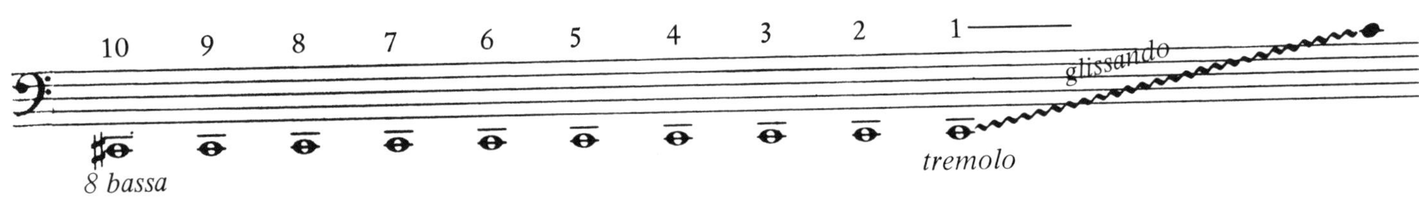

The next part, depicting the flight through space, is a whole-tone scale starting on middle C and moving upward three octaves. At that point, the right hand plays the three white keys while the left hand plays the three adjacent black keys. The teacher may play this passage over and over to simulate the continued flight through space.

Of course, we will need to talk to earth as we fly through space. The teacher can play
the sounds of the spaceship as two students (one high and the other low) play random notes
for their conversation.

As our ship approaches the moon, the music gets slower and slower until finally a
tone cluster indicates a soft landing on the moon.

The sound of random tones (including .tone clusters and glissandos) will depict the
feeling of weightlessness as we bounce and glide over the moon's surface. The children
should be encouraged to move around the room in a free response to the music. Also, let
them take turns supplying the musical effects for this. Notice the example here uses no
stems or indicated note values and is intended purely as a "point of departure." Let the
imagination have free rein to create new sounds and rhythms.

After visiting the moon and collecting some samples to take back to earth, we now move back into our spaceship for the return. The rocket engine gradually lifts us from the moon's surface and we begin our journey back. All ends well with a nice, soft landing in our backyard, and we jump out of the ship to greet our friends.

Tall Clock (page 11)

The steady tick-tock, tick-tock of the clock is the beat or pulse of this music. Numerous activities can be done with this song or on this theme. First, there is the possibility of children moving as they swing to the steady beat of the clock's pendulum. This can be varied by introducing the idea of small clocks that tick faster and larger clocks that tick according to the swing of the pendulum.

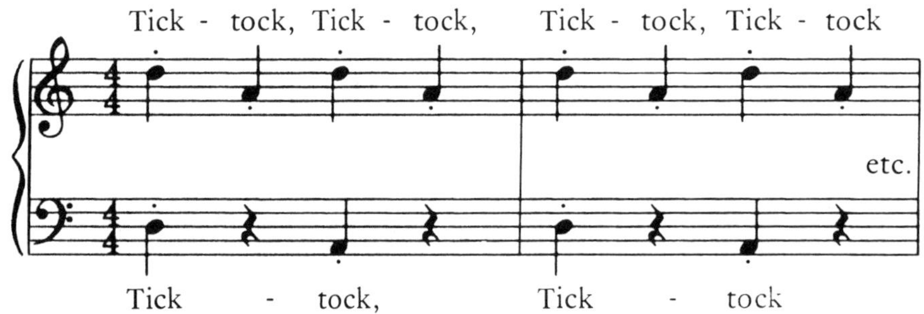

Also, you may explore the idea of chimes on clocks with big, deep sounds in contrast to the delicate, high chimes of others.

Use the words and choral speech of this song as a point of departure. At the end of the verse, a designated student may be the chime (by using the words "Bong! Bong!" as indicated here or actually playing the chime on a triangle, bell, or piano). The children do not have to sing the $G^\flat$, but rather chant (choral speech) at approximately that pitch.

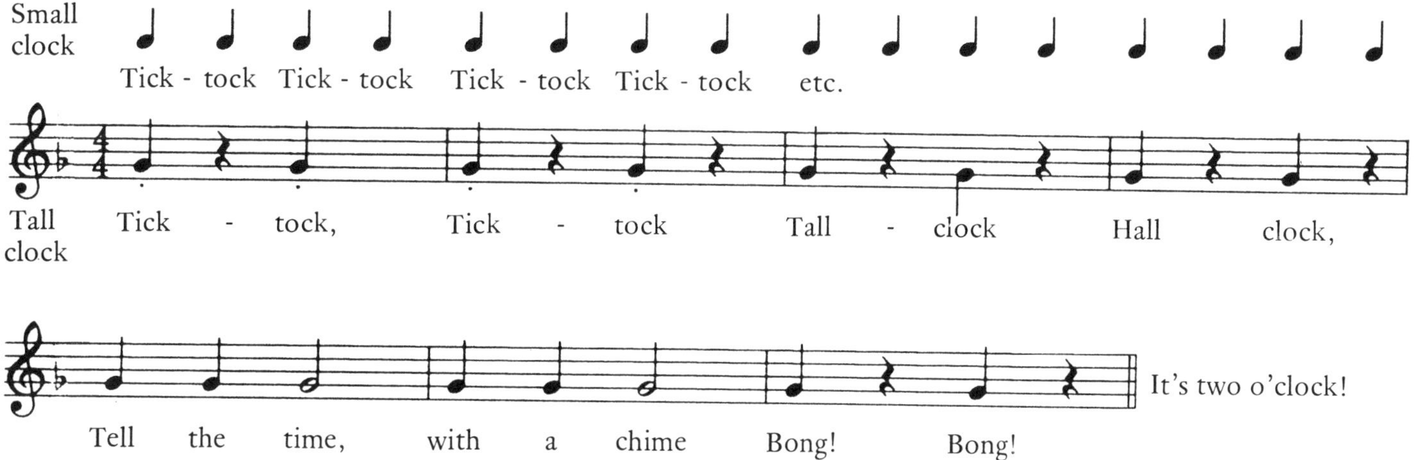

After the children know this song, you may wish to vary it further by using your hands to point the time on an imaginary clock and let the children guess the time by striking the "hour." Encourage the students to improvise new words and music to the steady ticking of the clock.

Musical Alphabet   (page 12)

It is important to continue regular drill on the musical alphabet until each student is totally at ease in identifying any note. Avoid using jingles or "crutches" -- they will only have to "unlearn" them eventually.

Cold and Frosty Mornin'   (page 13)

First sing this song to the children so they can enjoy the words! Sing and shape the melody since it is built on repeated tones that gradually ascend the first five notes of the scale, then descend quickly downward. Also, clap the rhythms as the students play the first beat of each measure with their pointer fingers. At the very end of this song, they can play all five tones down the scale. Also it is suggested that students transpose this to the keys of E and F major, as well as D major as written here.

Alabama Folk Song

Indian Song   (page 14)

The sounds of the pentatonic scale are heard in the music of many cultures throughout the world. Students should not get the idea that a pentatonic scale is only five black keys. It can be transposed to the white keys on either side or can actually be a different arrangement of the five tones. It is just that using the five black keys is an easy way to see and feel this five-tone scale.

The first example here is one in which the children may play either the melody or the drone bass on E^b and B^b. After they have the idea, they can create their own melodies in a similar mood. They should begin with a slow, whole-note ostinato in the bass. This can be varied by playing quarter notes in the last half of each bar or just four quarter notes.

Children should try making up their own "Indian" dances and improvise short melodies and sonorities for them. They can go from slow dances to quick ones as in the second example. Then they can return to the slower pattern to create a three-part form. At home the children can make up more pentatonic questions and answers with their parents.

Pentatonic Question and Answer (page 15)

The range and variety of creative activities -- particularly question and answer --
is literally unlimited. Here are just a few ideas for pentatonic questions and answers
in 2/4 .and 3/4 meter.

As students do their questions and answers each day, they should make up new questions, then create as many answers as possible. Encourage the use of the "drone" bass in the left hand for a stronger rhythm. If this creates a coordination problem, see if they can get another member of the family to play the left hand as the students do the questions and answers.

The Grand Staff   (page 16)

Review the ABCs on the keyboard, then introduce the treble and bass clefs, which together become the *grand staff*. Quickly put the three sequences of A to G on the chalkboard grand staff and let the students call out each letter name as you point to the various lines and spaces on the chalkboard. As time permits, draw a 𝄞 and 𝄢 with the students, then assign these to be done each day as part of their home practice. Be sure the students actually print the As, Bs, and Cs on the staff as a prerequisite for placing notes on the lines and spaces.

Don't let this become a "busy work" assignment -- rather, it should be enjoyable and a natural part of learning notation.

Dreaming   (page 17)

This song introduces the sound of the Dorian mode (D to D on the white keys). Although only five tones are used here, you can also play C to establish the Dorian sound. Let the students play *Dreaming* with one hand alone (either one), then show them how to create Dorian questions and answers. (By this time most students can coordinate the first, second, and third fingers of each hand -- some will be using all five.) Before changing to 2/4 or 4/4 meter, be sure they really feel the "swing" of questions and answers in 3/4. They may begin on any of the five white keys marked in the keyboard diagram and may also use the C below those marked.

In the long-range lesson planning, assignments using Dorian mode should be included every few weeks, interspersed with the new things as they appear in the book. In this way, the new ideas are gradually assimilated into the mental and technical processes of the student. Here are a few variants that add interest:

1) Begin on different tones and move by steps.
2) Use a motive that skips.
3) Use mostly repeated tones in the melody.
4) Play the question in one hand and the answer with the other.
5) See how many ways you can change the dynamics. For example, play two bars ⟨ and two bars ⟩ . Also, don't forget sudden changes in dynamics.
6) Change the meter and/or the tempo.
7) Change registers.

These variants can be applied to any other material in the book. Get students to use their imagination to become more creative individuals.

Flats (page 18)

As in previous examples, no finger numbers are suggested. Therefore students may use either 1, 2, and 3 of each hand or 1, 2, and 3 in the right hand and 5, 4, and 3 in the left hand. They should play each hand alone at first and only try both hands together if they have acquired the necessary skill.

Don't "over-explain" flats. Merely show that the flat lowers a tone to the next closest one, then proceed with a short keyboard drill.

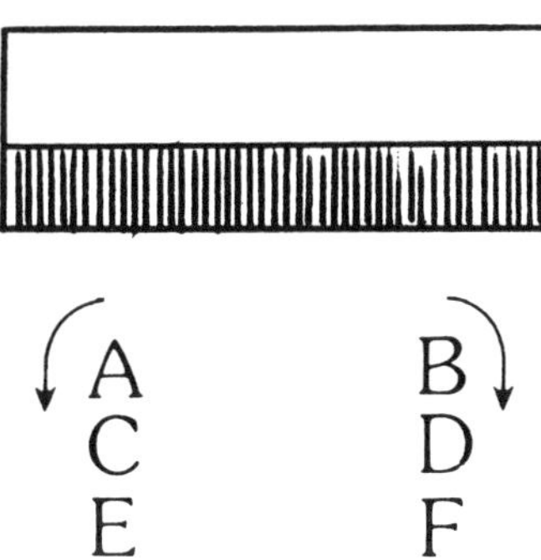

Let the students try this in pairs until each has had several turns.

Sharps (page 19)

The same teaching procedures apply in introducing sharps as they did in flats. Present both flats and sharps in the same lesson if possible. Keyboard drill should precede the actual making of the ♯ or ♭ at the chalkboard or on paper. Again, as the students play the melody, they should play each hand alone unless they have developed enough control to use both hands.

Do a few minutes of keyboard drill on flats and sharps for several weeks. Gradually do more blackboard drill as preparation for identifying key signatures.

Three Little Kittens (page 20)

This song introduces 6/8 meter with its two pulses per measure and emphasizes the relationship of the following:

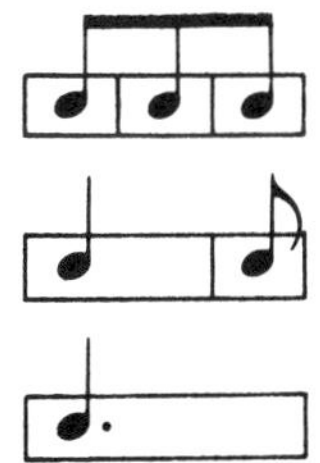

First sing the melody and clap the beat. Then sing it again as the students shape the melody in the air. This may be played by using three fingers of the right hand and the pointer finger of the left.

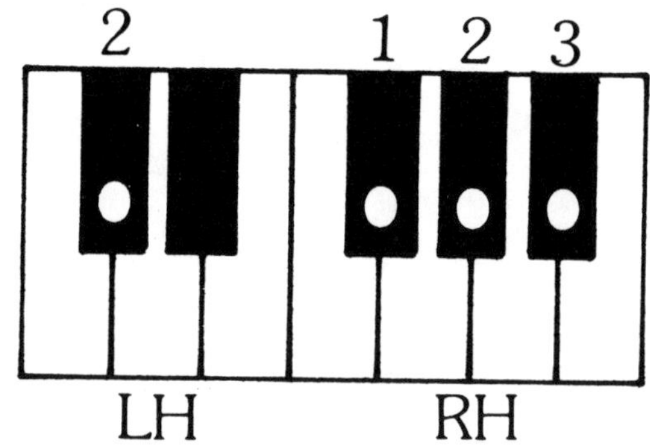

As the students sing and shape the melody, be sure they notice the repeated tones and skips. Also, let them find the one exception in each phrase where it moves by a step. Let them improvise new melodies for these words and also be sure they transpose up to G and down to F major.

Ralph (page 21)

Here is a song in minor with repeated notes, to be played in the bass clef. Be sure students feel the rhythm of the *short long note* (♩ ♩) in contrast to the *half note dot* (♩.). This may be played with either hand or by using the left hand on G and A and the right hand on B♭.

There are many possibilities for interesting stories about Ralph (pronounced Rrr-al-fff to simulate the deep sound of the big, green bullfrog).

Some ideas:

1) Ralph hops around the pond to visit his friends. (Hopping music.)
2) He quietly watches the big dragonfly in front of him. (Soft, low tones.) What will he do?
3) Ralph dives into the pond and visits Slippy Fish. (Free improvisation.)
4) Tim Turtle and Ralph play hide and seek with the little girl and her dog. (Make up a motif for each character.)

Other suggestions: Make up new words and melodies. Also introduce new characters.

Who's That? (page 22)

This three-note melody moves first by a skip, then the repeated notes move in a stepwise pattern. Use the names of the students in the class to answer the question "Who's that tapping at my window?" This can be transposed to a new key as new names are introduced. See how many names you can use (in turn, how many transpositions). Also, create new melodies using these words and the same rhythm.

Bingo   (page 23)

Bingo is a song that may be taught in stages. After singing and shaping the entire melody, the teacher can show the students how to play just the sequence B-I-N-G-O (the melodic pattern occurs three times). They can play this either with their pointer finger or as part of a four-note pattern for the right hand beginning with the third finger. Here are some of the "stages":

1) Sing the melody and shape it in the air.
2) Sing the melody as they clap the rhythm and walk the beat.
3) As mentioned above, play each "BINGO" pattern on the keyboard but just sing the opening and closing phrases.
4) One student plays the first four bars followed by three students each playing two bars (BINGO) and finally all join in singing the last two bars.

These are only a few ideas to try.

Big Machine   (page 24)

One of the primary considerations of this song is the sound of bitonality (illustrated by using white and black keys in the same song). This also provides an early experience with two-note tone clusters. Soon this can be expanded to three- and four-note clusters.

Additional creative activities for this song should include songs using high and low notes, new ostinatos, different melodic designs, and new tonal combinations. Make up short two-line verses with the children so they can create new melodies and several ostinatos. The question-and-answer phrase structure is excellent so that children can quickly make up several different examples then go on to something else in their assignment.

Question and Answer   (page 25)

This page is a study of sequence, inversion, and repetition. In the first question, point out the sequence that is answered by an inversion.

Let the students create answers both in this key and others such as E, G^b, and G major.

The next example presents repetition and sequences with passing tones. Continue to use these basic ideas for several weeks to realize the variety of experiences that can emanate from just two questions and answers.

Barnyard Song   (page 26)

There are several well-known melodies for these verses. Here is a new melody that emphasizes movement first by skips and then by "stepping" tones (see last five notes of the phrase). The second phrase also moves by skips with the exception of the very end. Let students improvise other new melodies by beginning on either the bottom or middle tone of the pattern. (Be sure to "shape" each new melody with the students to help visualize the melodic design.)

Students will love to add new verses for each animal or bird in the illustration, plus adding other verses for any other creatures which they may want to "invite" to come to "dinner."

Transpose this up and down to other keys.

Flats   (page 28)

Drill on flats and sharps should involve a few minutes at each lesson as well as daily practice at home. Students may play each tone, then say its name as they lower or raise it (say $A^{\#}$ or A^{b}, etc.). Teachers may draw out additional keyboards for students to mark if necessary. Be sure there is adequate keyboard drill on identifying these ABCs -- don't let it become merely a busy work assignment on paper.

Hop, Old Squirrel   (page 29)

Understanding both the melodic and the rhythmic patterns of this song are important to the musical development of the students. First, sing and shape the melody, then clap it as you walk the beat. Next, compare the three note groupings such as ♩ ♩ ♩ and ♫ ♩ . Children should discover that the tones of *Hop, old squirrel* are longer than the ones for *eidle-dum*. Find all repeated note groupings. What happens in the second measure of each score?

Mention that the sharps tell us to play these on the black keys. Compare the melody of the first and second lines. Finally, students can create their own new melodies to these words and transpose to adjacent keys.

Tune Up   (pages 30 and 31)

This is the first time the students are specifically called on to use all five fingers of either hand. Use the same procedures as on page 3 to present this. The "building block" outline of the melody will help to visualize both the melodic contour and also the rhythm. It is not important which hand is presented first. However, all students should use the same hand to avoid confusion over finger numbers.

Students should be aware of the all-white note pattern of C major, the black-black-white-black-black pattern of D^b major, and the reverse of this for D major. Now that this tune up has been introduced, it should be used for many weeks by students to orient themselves to the sound of any particular key. Do *Tune Up* as a game that students can play at home, i.e., "Can you tune up beginning on any key of the piano?"

Be sure that students transpose this to the remaining six keys -- G^b, G, A^b, A, B^b, and B major.

Grand Staff   (page 32)

The grand staff was first presented on page 16 (and letter names of the keyboard on page 8), and by this time students should have become well aware of note names. It has been a gradual process over a period of weeks rather than a big "push" at any point. The game aspect of keyboard drill on the ABCs peaks the students thereby motivating them to learn the letter names more quickly. Have them come to the piano in pairs as previously shown.

The same drill sequence is effective at the chalkboard to learn lines and spaces. First the teacher can point to the lines and/or spaces of either clef on the chalkboard as students call out the answers. This should be followed by students writing the letter names on each line or space. Also, flash cards are very helpful.

As indicated by the diagram on page 32, each letter name of the grand staff represents a definite pitch or place on the keyboard. Therefore, be sure to give students practice finding these until you are certain they can find any specific note.

Riding Along   (page 33)

Riding Along should be played first as a duet (one student plays the accompaniment as the other plays the melody). Then (if coordination permits) students may play the left-hand ostinato as they play the question and answer melody. Be sure to create new ones. They can also use this as an ostinato for the left hand.

Assign new questions and answers for both the pentatonic scale and also in the keys of F and G major (white keys).

Fire Truck   (page 34)

It is important to point out the relation of the repeated note pattern of the right hand melody to the tone cluster in the left-hand accompaniment. In the beginning, all can sing the melody as teacher or one student plays the tone-cluster accompaniment. Next, the teacher might play the melody as another student tries the tone clusters. Be sure to shape the melody and create new ones on the same keys.

For additional activities, play the song as one student (the fire truck) moves around the room and stops at the "home" of another student:

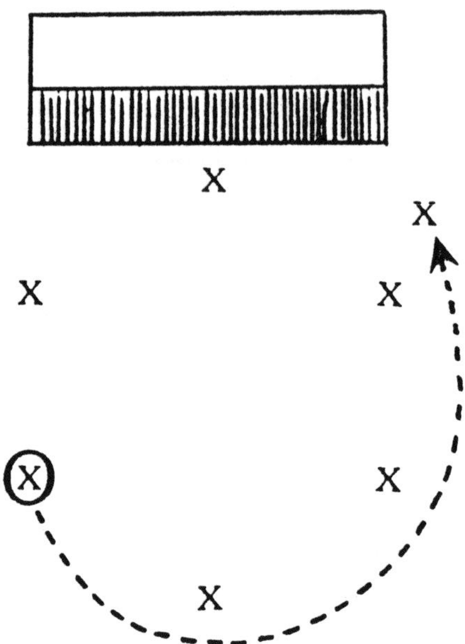

Then sing and play it again as the second student proceeds around the circle to the next "fire." This should be transposed to at least G^b and F major and can also be done bitonally (tone clusters in G and melody in G^b).

New verses and melodies will add even more interest and variety for home application.

Old Mr. Rabbit   (page 35)

First, teacher and students should shape this melody and clap the rhythm as they study the melodic contour and rhythmic patterns. Notice that the first line uses only two tones in a two-bar repeated rhythm. Two eighth notes (♫) are substituted in a third bar for the quarter note (♩) in the first bar. The first two bars of the second line consist of repeated notes and stepwise movement followed by skips in the last two bars.

The right hand can play all notes with the exception of the D in the last measure. Transpose to the black keys indicated ($F^\#$ or G^b) and to G major if time allows.

You can substitute the names of other vegetables at the end of the song to create other verses.

Muffin Man   (page 36)

This new melody for *Muffin Man* uses four of the five black keys of the pentatonic scale. Mention that the flats tell us to lower the tones to those black keys shown here. You can also play this on all white keys in F major, then transpose up to G major.

As students shape this melody, they should notice the skip, repeated tones, and stepwise movement. Let them create new melodies as they experiment with neighboring and passing tones such as these:

Also, they may use all five tones of the pentatonic scale.

Fill-In   (page 37)

For the first few weeks, the teacher can make dots on the chalkboard for the flats and sharps in the G^b and F$^\#$ major key signatures. Before long, however, tell students to take a "picture" of this in their minds. They should be made aware of the "shape" of

each key signature. Then let them make G^b and F$^\#$ major from memory. Flash cards as well as chalkboard drill greatly facilitate the learning of these two configurations. Don't bother with other key signatures yet. Let them first learn the placement for G^b and F$^\#$ major, then they can apply the appropriate rule to all other flat or sharp keys.

April Showers   (page 38)

April Showers is a good subject to inspire other songs about thunder (low tone clusters and rolled notes), rain drops (staccato notes), slipping in the mud (short glissando), to mention only a few ideas. Teacher and students should make up new words and melodies on the subject of April showers and May flowers. The rhythmic pulse of the songs can be carried by the "drip-drop" ostinato in the bass. Teacher can create the first new melody as one student plays the ostinato. Then the teacher should let students make up their new melodies as others take turns playing "drip-drop." At home, another member of the family can play the beat as the student plays first the original melody and then creates others.

Be sure the students see the repeated pattern of the first and second bars (three repeated notes and a skip). Next they should see that this same pattern recurs in the second phrase. Also, they should notice the skips in the third and fourth bars and compare these with the last two bars. This song is a good study of intervals (seconds, thirds, and fourths).

Sharps and Flats   (page 39)

Weeks of keyboard drill on the ABCs with their sharps and flats should precede the fill-ins on this page.

Quiet Time   (page 40)

This song in Phrygian mode (E to E on the white keys) should evoke some quietly unique melodies. First do this as a question and answer, using the same hand for both question and answer. Then experiment with the question in one hand and give the answer in the other. Try melodies beginning on the third or fifth tones and finally create new rhythms. Here are a few suggestions:

Questions   (page 41)

Two primary objectives of this page are to highlight both melodic shapes and rhythmic patterns. Students should "shape" the melody in the air as each question is being played. Then, as each student creates his or her answer, the rest of the group can try to shape it in the air. Make up new melodies in 3/4 meter and have students draw the contours of each on the board. For example:

Students should be aware that the melodic contour also indicates the rhythm (long and short lines).

Paw Paw Patch   (page 42)

This melody emphasizes repeated tones and skips as shown by the shadow boxes. Students should find all of the repeated tones, then look for the skips. Also, they should sing and shape the melody, then clap the rhythm as they sing it again.

Notice that the first two bars are played with the right hand, followed by two bars in the left hand. The melody of the last line is again played by the right hand. Notice that the right hand plays all white keys, but the left hand plays an F$^\#$.

It may be easier for students to play quarter rather than eighth notes in the next-to-last bar. The song should be transposed to F major and other keys as time permits. This becomes a good action song as other verses are added. For instance:

Picking up paw paws, puttin' them in a basket, etc.

(Students act as if they were picking them up and placing them in a basket.)

Tugboat   (page 43)

First play this song as written in the Phrygian mode (you can have students "tune up" from E to B with F natural to get the real sound), then transpose it down a step to play it in the Dorian mode. Compare this with *Quiet Time* on page 40 to see certain similarities and differences in the melody.

After presenting this as a song to be played entirely by one hand, let students play a question in the right hand then an answer in the left (or vice versa). Later, students can add one or both of the tones indicated on the keyboard for the left hand as an ostinato.

Make up new words and melodies for more songs about the little tugboat. At first students can use the same rhythm, but change the melodic design (start on the upper note and skip down). Later, they can change both the meter and rhythm to accommodate their new words.

Rosa   (page 44)

First sing and "swing" this melody with the students. Feel a strong two-beat pulse per measure. Once this "swing" is established, you can clap the rhythm and shape the melody in the air. Can they recognize the repetition in the second line? Also, can they find the sequence with the words "be dancing"?

After singing, clapping, and shaping this several times, let the students play the bass pattern of G, G, D, G with pointer fingers of both hands. Sing it again as some students provide the accompaniment. Then let someone play the melody as another student tries to keep the bass part going. Eventually, some may be able to do both parts. Don't forget to transpose as indicated.

Additional activities might include improvising new melodies for these words and transposing to Dorian and/or Phrygian modes.

Review   (page 45)

This page is a review of keyboard letter names plus their respective flats and sharps. Be sure there is ample keyboard drill before assigning the fill-ins on page 45. This page also gives students another encounter with key signatures. For the moment, just let them trace over the flats and sharps -- there is still plenty of time to present rules. You can also let them draw the six flats and six sharps on the chalkboard. Be sure to emphasize the pattern of the key signatures for both six flats and six sharps. See if the students have a picture of these in their minds.

The Fly and the Bumblebee   (page 46)

As with previous songs, students should shape the melody in the air as they sing it. They should also clap the rhythm and feel the two-pulse swing. They can also play it in the air as they wiggle each finger. This melody can be played entirely with one hand or the first measure with the right hand followed by the left hand in the second measure with either or both hands playing the last two measures.

After playing this in D major (notice no key signature is used -- rather, only $F^{\#}$ as needed), transpose to other keys.

Question and Answer   (page 47)

This page is a review of questions and answers in 3/4 and 4/4 meter. The first question and answer relates to earlier examples presented on pages 9 and 25 while the second question and answer, which is pentatonic, relates to page 15. Also see if students can identify the melodic similarities between page 17 and the question and answer on page 25. Be sure students create their own questions and answers.

Now the students have completed this book and are ready to read musical notation, create their own music, and begin to notate what they see and hear. They have *experienced, discovered,* and *explored* some of the "basics," which will help them make and enjoy music via the piano and they have acquired certain necessary prerequisites for further musical learning.

It is important that the upward learning spiral be continued through an interrelated instructional program of harmony, ear-training, sightreading, transposition, improvisation, repertoire, and technique. This must include microcosms of all styles and periods of keyboard music that are presented in a well-organized, structured sequence. Students have a better chance of learning when both teaching techniques and materials are organized in a meaningful way.

STUDIO POLICY
and
RESERVATION FORM

Please enroll ____ for piano instruction in
the ______________________ studio, beginning ____________________, 19____ .

I understand the policy of the studio, which is:

1) The course of instruction will cover 36 weeks, to include a minimum of two,
    45-minute classes per week for the child, and one open class (approximately
    every six weeks) for the parents to attend with their child.

2) No lessons are scheduled during the following vacations or holidays:

        Thanksgiving   Easter
        Christmas   Memorial Day

3) There will be no refund for missed lessons. Make-up lessons will be given
    ONLY in the case of extended illness. However, a new lesson assignment will
    be prepared and mailed to the absent student immediately and the full lesson
    time will be given to the partner.

4) Tuition for the course is ___________________, payable in three installments
    of ________________ each, due:

        September 1, 19___
        January 1,   19___
        April 1,   19___

5) No lessons can be attended without receipt of current payment. Tuition is
    refundable ONLY in the event that a family moves to another location. Other-
    wise the student is enrolled for the entire course of study.

6) Books, sheet music, and supplies are not included in the tuition, but will be
    billed at the time tuition is due.

7) A regular practice schedule is vitally important to the success of the student,
    so daily practice forms should be properly filled out.

8) There must be a well-tuned piano available for daily use. (One tuning per
    year is recommended.)

9) Enclosed is _________ our non-refundable enrollment deposit, which will be
    credited to the third payment of tuition. The deposit is due June 1, 19___ .
    No reservation can be made without this registration fee.

        (Parent's signature) ____

        (Address) ____

                  ____

Please retain one copy for your files and return one copy by ____________________